and Answers

Carine Mackenzie

CF4•K

© Copyright 2001 Carine Mackenzie
ISBN: 978-1-85792-570-8
Reprinted in 2002, 2004, 2005, 2007
and 2008 (twice), 2009, 2010
by Christian Focus Publications,
Geanies House, Fearn,
Ross-shire, IV20 1TW,
Great Britain.

The Scripture quotations in this book are based on the
New King James version of the scriptures.

www.christianfocus.com
email:info@christianfocus.com

Cover design by A Macinnes and
Daniel van Straaten
All illustrations by Diane Mathes

Printed and bound by Bell and Bain, Glasgow

Mixed Sources
Product group from well-managed
forests and other controlled sources
www.fsc.org   Cert no. TT-COC-002769
© 1996 Forest Stewardship Council

Contents

RECOMMENDATION

As evangelicals, we have analysed the harmful cultural influences on our children but have been less effective in offering positive solutions to the problem. It is a joy, therefore, to recommend very highly Carine Mackenzie's new Catechism for children.

Here is something that Christian parents, grandparents and friends can do for the character development and wholesome spiritual growth of the young generation: teach them this catechism!

It is Biblically sound throughout; a fine and clear summation of the structure of Reformed Theology. It is both comprehensive and comprehensible. Written in very plain and current English, it wastes no words and keeps to the point at issue in each question, and is organized so that theological concepts follow each other in proper order, much like its model, the Westminster Shorter Catechism.

It presents profound truth as simply as possible. As a father of five, I deem it to be happily accessible to children. It conveys a spirit of uplifting devotion.

This catechism could make a great difference in the lives of those who learn it. My prayer is that it may be very widely read.

DOUGLAS F. KELLY,
RTS CHARLOTTE

RECOMMENDATION

ruth, clarity, and simplicity are the great virtues of this God-exalting catechism for children. It was a great pleasure to watch our daughter learn these answers. As usual, teaching a child great truths about God enriched our own thinking and intensified our own worship.

JOHN AND NOEL PIPER

1. God

1. Who made you?
   God.
   Genesis 1:27.

2. Why did God make you?
   To glorify him and enjoy him.
   1 Corinthians 10:31.

3. **What else did God make?**
God made all things.
Genesis 1:31.

4. **Why did God make all things?**
For his own glory.
Revelation 4:11.

5. **Where does God teach us to praise and enjoy him?**
In his Word, the Bible.
John 5:39.

6. **Who wrote the Bible?**
Holy men who were taught by the Holy Spirit.
2 Timothy 3:16.

7

7. **What is God?**
God is a spirit.
John 4:24.

8. **What is a spirit?**
An invisible being
who does not have a
body like us.
Colossians 1:15.

9. **Where is God?**
God is everywhere.
Job 11:7.

10. **Did God have a beginning?**
No. He has always existed.
Psalm 90:2.

11. **Will he have an end?**
No. He will always exist.
Psalm 102:27.

12. **Does God ever change?**
    No. He is always the same.
    Psalm 102:27.

13. **Does God know everything?**
    Yes. Nothing can be hidden from him.
    Psalm 44:21.

14. **Can God do everything?**
    Yes. He can do everything that pleases him.
    Isaiah 40:13.

15. **Can you see God?**

No.
I cannot see God but he always sees me.
Colossians 1.15.

16. **How many Gods are there?**

There is only one God.
Isaiah 45:5.
Deuteronomy 6:4.

17. **How many persons are there in the one God?**

Three persons.
Matthew 28:19.

18. **Who are these three persons?**

The Father, the Son and the Holy Spirit.
Matthew 28:19.

2. Creation

19.   Who made the world?
        God.
        Genesis 1:31.

20.   Did God make the world out
        of something?
        No. There was nothing else before
        the world.
        Hebrews 11:3.

21.   How did God make the
        world?
        By speaking powerful words.
        Psalm 148:5.

22. How long did it take?

Six days.
Genesis 1:1-31.

23. What did God do on the seventh day?

He rested and made the seventh day of the week his special day.
Genesis 2:2.

24. Who was the first man God made?

Adam.
Genesis 5:2.

25. Who was the first woman that God made?

Eve.
Genesis 3:20.

26. What did God make Adam from?

The dust of the ground.
Genesis 2:7.

27. What did God make Eve from?

One of Adam's ribs.
Genesis 2:22.

28. What did God give to Adam and Eve as well as bodies?

He gave them souls that would never die.

Genesis 2:7.

29. Do you have a soul as well as a body?

Yes. I have a soul that will never die.

Matthew 16:26.

30. How do you know that you have a soul?

Because God tells me so in the Bible.

Psalm 121:7.

3. How Man Sinned

31. Were Adam and Eve good when God made them?

Yes, very good. All that God made was good.
Genesis 1:31.

32. What is sin?

Sin is disobeying or not keeping God's law in any way.
Romans 5:12.

33. What is disobeying God's law?

Doing what God says not to do.
Luke 22:61.

34. **What is not keeping God's law?**

Not being or doing what God requires.

Luke 10:31.

35. **Did Adam and Eve continue to be good?**

No. They sinned by disobeying God.

Genesis 3:3.

36. **How did Adam and Eve sin?**

By eating fruit that God had said not to eat.

Genesis 3:6.

4. What happened because of Sin?

37. **What happened to Adam and Eve when they sinned?**

    They were separated from God.
    Genesis 3:24.

38. **Does Adam's sin affect us?**

    Yes. We are all Adam's children. He acted for us all and as a result we are all born in a sinful condition.
    Romans 5:12.

39. **What name do we give to this sinful condition?**

    Original sin.
    Romans 7:23.

40. **What other sin are we guilty of as well as original sin?**

Actual sin in what we do, say and think.

Matthew 15:19.

41. **What does every sin deserve?**

God's anger and punishment.

Isaiah 59:2.

42. **Can anyone go to heaven with this sinful condition?**

No. Our hearts must be changed before we can be fit for heaven.

Psalm 9:17.

5. Salvation

43.   What did God do to save his people from his anger and punishment?

He sent his Son so that whoever believes in him would not perish but have everlasting life.

John 3:16.

44.   Who is God's Son?

The Lord Jesus Christ.

Luke 1:35.

45.   How did he come to this world?

He was born in Bethlehem in a stable.

Luke 2:4-7.

46. **Who was his mother?**

The virgin Mary.
Matthew 1:18.

47. **Did he have an earthly father?**

No. He came into the world by the power of the Holy Spirit.
Matthew 1:18.

48. **Why did he come in this way?**

So that he would be free from original sin.
Hebrews 7:26.

49. Did Jesus ever commit any sin?

No. He obeyed God perfectly always.

Hebrews 4:15.

50. Why was God's Son given the name Jesus?

Jesus means Saviour and he saves his people from their sins.

Matthew 1:21.

51. How did Jesus save his people from their sin?

Jesus Christ suffered and died in the place of his people to pay the price for all their sins.

Hebrews 9:28.

52. **For whom did Jesus suffer and die?**
For all the people that God the Father gave him.
John 6:44-45.

53. **Who will be saved?**
Only those who repent of their sins and believe in Jesus Christ.

Mark 1:15.

54. **What does it mean to repent of your sin?**
I am truly sorry for my sins. I hate them and want to stop doing them. I want to live to please God.
Isaiah 1:16-17.

55. Can you decide to repent and believe in Jesus on your own?

No. I can only do so with the help of the Holy Spirit.
Romans 2:4.

56. How can you get the Holy Spirit's help?

By praying to God to give me his help.
Luke 11:13.

57. How were people saved who lived before Christ died?

They believed in the Saviour that God would send.
Romans 4:3.

6. Jesus as Prophet, Priest and King

58. In what different ways did Jesus fulfil Old Testament promises about himself?

He came to be a prophet, a priest and a king.

Acts 3:22.

Hebrews 5:6.

Psalm 2:6.

59. How is Christ our prophet?

He teaches us the will of God.

John 16:13.

60. How is Christ our priest?

We are guilty of sin and he has died as a sacrifice for the sins of his people. Now that he has risen and ascended, he continually prays for them.

Colossians 1:20.

61. How is Christ our king?

He rules the world and defends his people from Satan, the evil one.

2 Corinthians 10:5.

7. The Ten Commandments

62. How many commandments did God give on Mount Sinai?

Ten commandments.
Exodus 20:3-17.

63. What do the commandments 1-4 tell us?

How to love God.
Exodus 20:3-11.

64. What do the commandments 5-10 tell us?

How to love other people.
Exodus 20:12-17.

65. **What is the summary of the ten commandments?**

To love the Lord our God with all our heart, and soul and strength and mind, and to love our neighbour as we love ourselves.

Matthew 22:37-40.

66. **Who is our neighbour?**

Every human being.
Luke 10:36.

8. The First Commandment

67. **What is the first commandment?**

    The first commandment is,
    You shall have no other gods
    before me.
    Exodus 20:3.

68. **What does the first commandment teach us?**

    To worship God only.
    1 Chronicles 28:9.

9. The Second Commandment

69. ## What is the second commandment?

The second commandment is, You shall not make for yourself an idol in the form of anything in heaven above or on the earth beneath or in the waters below. You shall not bow down to them or worship them; for I the Lord your God am a jealous God, punishing the children for the sin of the fathers to the third and fourth generations of those who hate me, but showing love to a thousand generations of those who love me and keep my commandments.

Exodus 20:4-6.

70. **What does the second commandment tell us to do?**

To worship God in the way that he tells us in his word, and not to use man-made idols or statues. Deuteronomy 12:32.

10. The Third Commandment

71.   What is the third commandment?

The third commandment is, You shall not misuse the name of the Lord your God, for the Lord will not hold anyone guiltless who misuses his name.

Exodus 20:7.

72.   What does the third commandment tell us to do?

To honour God's name and not to use God's name in a careless way.
Psalm 29:2.

11. The Fourth Commandment

73. **What is the fourth commandment?**

The fourth commandment is, Remember the Sabbath day by keeping it holy. Six days you shall labour and do all your work, but the seventh day is a Sabbath to the Lord your God. On it you shall not do any work, neither you, nor your son or daughter, nor your manservant or maidservant, nor

your animals, nor the foreigners who live in your towns. For in six days the Lord made the heavens and the earth, the sea and all that is in them, but he rested on the seventh day. Therefore the Lord blessed the Sabbath day and made it holy.
Exodus 20:8-11.

74. **What does the fourth commandment tell us?**

To keep the Sabbath holy.
Leviticus 19:30.

75. **What day of the week is the Christian Sabbath?**

The first day of the week or Lord's Day on which Christ rose from the dead.
Acts 20:7.
Revelation 1:10.

76. **What should we do on the Sabbath?**

We should worship God with his people and on our own, pray to him, praise him, read or listen to his Word and do good to other people.
Isaiah 58:13-14.

12. The Fifth Commandment

77. **What is the fifth commandment?**

The fifth commandment is, Honour your father and mother, so that you may live long in the land the Lord your God is giving you.
Exodus 20:12.

78. **What does the fifth commandment tell us to do?**

To love and obey our parents and all people in authority over us.
Colossians 3:20.

13. The Sixth Commandment

79. **What is the sixth commandment?**

   The sixth commandment is, You shall not murder.
   Exodus 20:13.

80. **What does the sixth commandment tell us to do?**

   Not to take the life of another or to fight with anyone.
   Psalm 82:3-4.
   Matthew 5:21-22.

14. The Seventh Commandment

81.   What is the seventh commandment?

The seventh commandment is, You shall not commit adultery. Exodus 20:14.

82.   What does the seventh commandment tell us to do?

To be pure in our thoughts, words and behaviour. 2 Timothy 2:22.

15. The Eighth Commandment

83. **What is the eighth commandment?**

   The eighth commandment is,
   You shall not steal.

   Exodus 20:15.

84. **What does the eighth commandment tell us to do?**

   To be honest and to work hard to look after ourselves and others, and to respect the property of others.

   Romans 12:17.

16. The Ninth Commandment

85. What is the ninth commandment?

The ninth commandment is,
You shall not give false testimony
against your neighbour.
Exodus 20:16.

86. What does the ninth commandment tell us to do?

To tell the truth at all times.
Zechariah 8:16.

17. The Tenth Commandment

87.   What is the tenth commandment?

The tenth commandment is, You shall not covet your neighbour's house. You shall not covet your neighbour's wife, or his manservant or maidservant, his ox or donkey, or anything that belongs to your neighbour.
Exodus 20:17.

88.   What does the tenth commandment tell us to do?

To be content with what we have and not to be envious of others.
1 Timothy 6:8.

18. Keeping God's Laws

89.   Can we obey the ten commandments perfectly?

No. We break them every day in thought, word and deed.
Psalm 14:3.

90.   Has anyone ever perfectly obeyed the ten commandments?

Only the Lord Jesus Christ, who is God and man in one person, has perfectly obeyed the ten commandments.
Hebrews 4:15, 1 Peter 2:22.

91.   What do we deserve for breaking the commandments?

God's anger and punishment.
Romans 6:23.

19. The Way to be Saved

92. How can we escape from God's anger and punishment?

God, in his mercy, has provided the only way of escape through faith in the Lord Jesus Christ for those who repent.
Acts 20:21.

93. What is faith?

Faith in Jesus Christ is a gift from God, when we trust in him completely to save us from sin.
John 3:16.

94. What is repentance?

Repentance is a gift from God. We are made to be truly sorry for our sins. We turn from them to Jesus Christ. We live to please him.

Luke 18:13.

20. Experiencing God's Salvation

95. How does God help us to experience his salvation?

By his Word, the Bible, the sacraments and prayer.
Acts 2:42.
2 Timothy 3:15.

96. How should we read the Word?

We should read the Bible carefully and believe all of it.
2 Timothy 3:16.

21. Baptism and the Lord's Supper

97. **What are the sacraments of the church?**

   The sacraments are Baptism and the Lord's Supper.

   Matthew 28:19-20.

98. **What is Baptism?**

   Baptism is the outward sign of washing with water, in the name of the Father, and of the Son and of the Holy Spirit, which tells us about the cleansing from sin by the blood of Jesus Christ and about belonging to God.

   Acts 2:38-41.

99. **What is the Lord's Supper?**

The Lord's Supper is the outward sign of eating bread and drinking wine which tells us about the death of the Lord Jesus Christ for his people.

1 Corinthians 11:23.

100. **What do the bread and wine represent?**

The body of Christ and the blood of Christ.

1 Corinthians 11:24-25.

101. **Why did Jesus Christ command this sacrament to be kept by those who trust in him?**

So that his suffering and death would be remembered and proclaimed till the end of the world.

1 Corinthians 11:26.

22. Prayer

102. What is prayer?
Prayer is asking God for things that are agreeable to him, confessing our sins to him and thanking him for all his mercies.
Philippians 4:6.

103. In whose name should we pray?
In the name of Jesus Christ.
John 16:23.

104. What has God given us to teach us to pray?
The whole Bible teaches us about prayer but Jesus especially teaches us about it in the Lord's Prayer.
Matthew 6:9-13.

105. What is the Lord's Prayer?

The Lord's Prayer is:-

Our Father in heaven,
Hallowed be your name.
Your kingdom come.
Your will be done on earth as it is
in heaven.
Give us today our daily bread.
Forgive us our debts as we also
have forgiven our debtors.
And lead us not into temptation
but deliver us from evil.
For yours is the kingdom and the
power and the glory forever.
Amen.

Matthew 6:9-13.

23. Where is Jesus Now?

106   Did Christ stay in the grave after he died?

No. He rose from the dead on the third day.

Matthew 28:6.

107.   Where is Christ now?

He is in heaven, sitting at the right hand of God the Father, praying always for his people.

Mark 16:19.

108.   Will he come to the world again?

Yes. At the end of time, Christ will come to judge the world.

Matthew 25:31-32.

24. Death

109.   What happens when a person dies?

The body decays but the soul lives on and goes either to heaven or to hell.

1 Thessalonians 4:14.

110.   Will the bodies of the dead be raised again?

Yes. When Christ returns, the bodies of the dead will be raised and joined to their souls forever. 1 Corinthians 15:43.

25. Hell

111. Where does God send the wicked?

To hell.
Matthew 25:41.

112. What is hell?

A terrible place of torment and punishment.
Luke 16:28.

26. Heaven

113.   Where does the godly person go at death?
To heaven.
Matthew 25:34.

114.   What is heaven?
A glorious joyful place where Christ is.
Revelation 21:4.

From the Author

Children of past generations were brought up with the immense benefit of learning the Shorter Catechism. A basic knowledge of Christian doctrine is vital in our day too.

This simple summary of some of the essentials of the faith compiled as a set of questions and answers is aimed at helping a young child learn what everyone needs to know.

In writing this, I found the Shorter Catechism and Willison's Mother's Catechism of immense help in deciding on a structure and what to include.

The learning of doctrine is not salvation but a good foundation of truth is valuable in combating false ideas which so easily divert young minds. Remember God's promise to his people, "I will put my laws in their minds and write them on their hearts."

Teaching the children is our responsibility. Applying that truth to the child's heart is the Lord's work.

CARINE MACKENZIE
AUTHOR

More Commendations

'Giving our children basic instruction in the faith is one of the primary responsibilities we have as Christian parents. Using this Children's Catechism is an ideal way of doing this. Here are the essential questions with the single-sentence, easily-remembered answers. This is God-centred, Christ-honouring, life-transforming, character-building teaching - a long term investment in a few pages.'

SINCLAIR B. FERGUSON

'The doctrines of Scripture in contemporary language that is easy to memorize. This book is an effective, foundational tool for godly parents to use in catechizing their children.'

JOEL BEEKE

'This new children's catechism is quite remarkable. It clearly articulates important doctrines in a manner that is clear yet without any compromising of the essential truths that parents need to teach their children. Sadly, the present generation has virtually lost the older practice of catechizing little ones. This much needed resource could go a long way in correcting this problem by providing a useable and simple tool for serious Christian parents to use.'

JOHN ARMSTRONG

'I heartily commend this children's catechism.'

R C SPROUL

Memory record

Tick each book once you have learned the question and the answer. There are 114 of them.

1	12	23
2	13	24
3	14	25
4	15	26
5	16	27
6	17	28
7	18	29
8	19	30
9	20	31
10	21	32
11	22	33

Memory record

34 46 58
35 47 59
36 48 60
37 49 61
38 50 62
39 51 63
40 52 64
41 53 65
42 54 66
43 55 67
44 56 68
45 57 69

Memory record

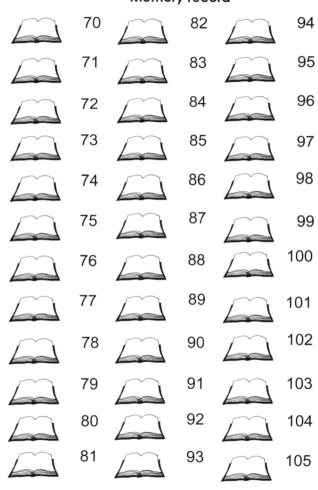

70
71
72
73
74
75
76
77
78
79
80
81

82
83
84
85
86
87
88
89
90
91
92
93

94
95
96
97
98
99
100
101
102
103
104
105

Memory record

106

109

112

107

110

113

108

111

114

IF YOU LIKED THIS YOU'LL LOVE THESE

My 1st Book of Bible Prayers, Philip Ross
ISBN: 978-1-85792-944-7

My 1st Book of Bible Promises, Carine Mackenzie
ISBN: 978-1-84550-039-9

My 1st Book of Christian Values, Carine Mackenzie
ISBN: 978-1-84550-262-1

My 1st Book of Memory Verses
Carine Mackenzie
ISBN: 978-1-85792-783-2

Bible Questions and Answers Teacher's Guide
Diana Kleyn
ISBN: 978-1-85792-701-6

For Older Children by Diana Kleyn and Joel Beeke

The Truth of God's Word Student Catechism
ISBN: 978-1-89277-723-2

Teacher's Manuel
ISBN: 978-1-89277-762-1

My 1st Book

of Bible Prayers

Philip Ross

FOR FAMILY DEVOTIONAL TIMES

The Big Book of Questions and Answers
Sinclair B Ferguson
ISBN: 978-1-85792-295-0

The Big Book of Questions and Answers about Jes
Sinclair B Ferguson
ISBN: 978-1-85792-559-3

Grandpa Mike Talks About God
Michael S. Lawson
ISBN: 978-1-84550-250-8

Read with Me
Jean Stapleton
ISBN: 978-1-84550-148-8

Children's Devotions
Frances Ridley Havergal
ISBN: 978-1-85792-973-7

God's Wisdom
Belinda Buckland
ISBN: 978-1-85792-963-8

Read
with me

365 Family Readings Giving
An Overview Of The Bible

Jean Stapleton

CHRISTIAN FOCUS PUBLICATIONS

Christian Focus | Christian Heritage | CF4K | Mentor

Christian Focus Publications publishes books for adults and children under its four main imprints: Christian Focus, Christian Heritage, CF4K and Mentor. Our books reflect that God's word is reliable and Jesus is the way to know him, and live for ever with him.

Our children's publication list includes a Sunday school curriculum that covers pre-school to early teens; puzzle and activity books. We also publish personal and family devotional titles, biographies and inspirational stories that children will love.

If you are looking for quality Bible teaching for children then we have an excellent range of Bible story and age specific theological books.

From pre-school to teenage fiction, we have it covered!

Find us at our web page:
www.christianfocus.com

CF4•K
Because you're never too young to know Jesus